A special

To

_____

From

_____

"**Curiosity** killed the cat

but for a while I was a suspect."

— Steven Wright

A kiss is a pleasant reminder that ***two*** heads are better than ***one***.''

— Unknown

A-RAGS-TO RICHES STORY

At the end of World War I, an American corporal stationed in Germany named Lee Duncan was on a scouting mission when he found a German shepherd and her five puppies that had been abandoned by the German army. Duncan and the other members of his patrol brought the little canine family back to their hangar, feeding and caring for them.

When he returned to the United States, Duncan brought two of the puppies with him. Within a few years, the male shepherd of the pair was making an income of $1000 a week, had his own personal chef, chauffeur and limousine, and a diamond-studded collar. Far from his humble beginning (both literally and figuratively), he became a top box-office star, and his name was widely known. He was, of course, Rin Tin Tin, and he made over 40 movies before his retirement in 1931.

You have to color outside the
lines once in a while if
you want to make your
life a masterpiece."

— Albert Einstein

"Be ready when opportunity comes. . .
Luck is the time when PREPARATION
and OPPORTUNITY meet."

— Roy D. Chapin, Jr.

Only dreamers can

teach us to soar."

— Anne Marie Pierce

"Life is like a wave,
some will catch it
and others will bail out."

— Unknown

"I long to accomplish a great and noble task; but it is my chief duty to accomplish small tasks as if they were **GREAT** and **NOBLE**."

— Helen Keller

THE MOST USEFUL DOG

A nursery school teacher was delivering a station wagon full of kids home one day when a fire truck zoomed past. Sitting in the front seat of the fire truck was a Dalmatian dog. The children fell to discussing the dog's duties. "They use him to keep crowds back," said one youngster.

"No," said another, "he's just for good luck."

A third child brought the argument to a close. "They use the dogs," she said firmly, "to find the fire hydrant."

Dogs are quick to show their affection. They never pout, they never bear a grudge. They never run away from home when mistreated. They never complain about their food. They never gripe about the way the house is kept. They are chivalrous and courageous, ready to protect their mistress at the risk of their lives. They love children, and no matter how noisy and boisterous they are, the dog loves every minute of it. In fact, a dog is still competition for a husband. Perhaps if we husbands imitated a few of our dogs' virtues, life with our family might be more amiable."

— Billy Graham

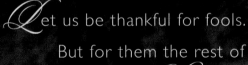

"Let us be thankful for fools. But for them the rest of us could not Succeed."

— Mark Twain

*Whoever is happy
will make others happy too."*

— Anne Frank

. . .Inasmuch as ye have done it unto the least of these my brethren, ye have done it unto me. – Matt. 25:40

Dear Lord, please make me
the person my dog thinks I am."

— Unknown

A true hero is not measured
by the size of his strength,
but by the strength of his *heart*."

— Unknown

HERO

The best and most beautiful things cannot be seen or touched.

They must be felt with the heart."

— Helen Keller

I will both lay me down in peace, and sleep: for thou, LORD, only makest me dwell in safety. – Ps. 4:8

"It is easy to sit up and take *notice*.

What is difficult is getting up and taking *action*."

— Al Batt

Rest in the LORD, and wait patiently for him ... – Ps. 37:7

The First Seeing-Eye Dog in America

Dorothy Harrison Eustis was a wealthy Philadelphian living in Switzerland at the end of World War I. After visiting a school in Pottsdam, Germany, that trained German shepherds as guides for blinded veterans of the war, she began training her own dogs to be guides. She was asked to write an article for the *Saturday Evening Post*, which appeared in the magazine in 1927.

A blind man named Morris Frank, living in Nashville, Tennessee, heard the article and wrote to Dorothy, asking her to train a dog for him. He said that if she would help him, he would start a dog-guide school in the United States to help others. She replied that she would grant his request if he would come to Switzerland to learn the training. He did travel there in 1928, learned how to train the dogs, and came home with Buddy, a female German shepherd, the first guide dog for the blind in America.

With a ten-thousand-dollar grant from Mrs. Eustis, Morris Frank established "The Seeing Eye" in 1929, the first dog-guide school in the United States. The school's name came from Proverbs

10:12, "The seeing eye, the hearing ear; the Lord hath made them both." (Only dogs trained at this school can be officially called "Seeing Eye dogs." The generic term is "dog guide.")

Seventeen dogs were trained in the first year, and Morris's mother, also blind, was one of the first recipients. The school is still in operation today, located in New Jersey.

"Imitation is the sincerest form of *flattery*."

— Charles Caleb Colton

Women and *cats* will do as they please,
and men and dogs should relax
and get used to the idea."

— Robert A. Heinlein

Commit thy way unto the LORD; trust also in him . . . – Ps. 37:5

To be loved,

be lovable.

— Ovid

. . . Love thy neighbor as thyself – Matt. 22:39

Being happy doesn't mean everything

is perfect. It means you have decided

to look beyond the imperfections."

— Unknown